A Kid's Guide to
INCREDIBLE TECHNOLOGY™

The Incredible Story of Jets

Greg Roza

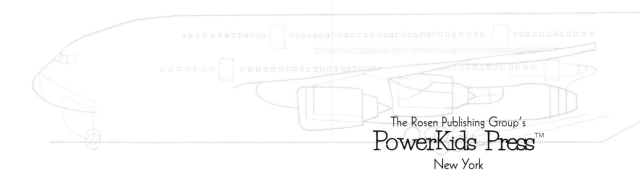

The Rosen Publishing Group's
PowerKids Press™
New York

For Shelby

Published in 2004 by The Rosen Publishing Group, Inc.
29 East 21st Street, New York, NY 10010

First Edition

Editor: Kathy Kuhtz Campbell
Book Design: Mike Donnellan

Illustration Credits: Alessandro Bartolozzi, Leonello Calvetti, Lorenzo Cecchi
Photo Credits: p. 4 © National Air and Space Museum, Smithsonian Institution, Washington, D.C. (SI Neg. No. 80—4267); p. 11 (left and right) © Bohemian Nomad Picturemakers/CORBIS; p. 15 © Philip Wallick/CORBIS; p. 16 (left) © Museum of Flight/CORBIS; p. 16 (right) © George Hall/CORBIS; p. 19 © Reuters NewMedia Inc./CORBIS.

Roza, Greg.
The incredible story of jets / Greg Roza.
    v. cm.— (A kid's guide to incredible technology)
Includes bibliographical references and index.
Contents: The history of flight—The forces of flight—Wings—Flaps, slats, ailerons, and rudders—Jet engines—Turbofans and turboprops—The Concorde—Big, bigger . . .—Biggest!—Let's get high-tech.
  ISBN 0-8239-6713-1 (library binding)
1. Jet planes—Juvenile literature. 2. Aeronautics—Juvenile literature. [1. Jet planes. 2. Aeronautics.] I. Title. II. Series.
  TL709 .R63 2004
  629.133′349—dc21
                                    2002015613

Manufactured in the United States of America

Contents

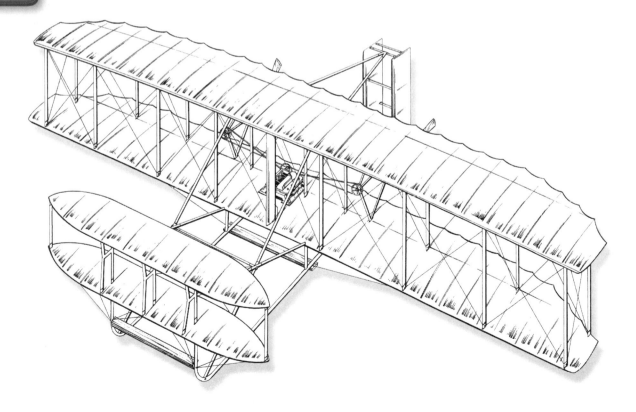

The History of Flight

On December 17, 1903, American brothers Orville and Wilbur Wright made the first successful airplane flight near Kitty Hawk, North Carolina. The flight lasted for 12 seconds and covered a distance of 120 feet (36.6 m). Since then, scientists and inventors have come a long way in understanding flight. They have improved the **technology** so much that some airplanes have a **wingspan** longer than the distance of the Wrights' flight! One of the greatest changes was the jet engine. Airplanes with jet engines are faster and more powerful than airplanes with **propellers**. Two men working in different places invented the jet engine around the same time. Frank Whittle of England filed a **patent** for his jet engine in 1930. However, Hans von Ohain of Germany built the first working jet engine in 1937.

Top: The Heinkel He-178 had a jet engine made by Hans von Ohain. The wingspan of the He-178 was 23 ¼ feet (7.1 m). Bottom: The Wrights' 1903 Flyer, seen here in a drawing, had a wingspan of 40 ⅓ feet (12.3 m).

The Forces of Flight

A Boeing 747 airplane can weigh up to 875,000 pounds (396,893.3 kg)! How does it stay in the air? To answer this question, we need to understand the forces of flight.

To get off the ground, an airplane must overcome its weight. The force that allows a plane to get off the ground is called lift. An airplane can rise into the sky only when the force of lift is greater than the plane's weight. **Thrust** is the force that moves an airplane forward. A plane creates thrust with its propellers or engines. The heavier the plane, the more effort it must put forth to get off the ground and to stay in the air. Thrust overcomes a force called **drag**. Drag resists, or goes against, the motion of an object as the object tries to move through a gas or a liquid. When the forces of thrust and drag are equal, a plane flies at an even rate of speed.

Top: *When you blow up a balloon, you create thrust. The squeezed air inside the balloon has force. Let go of the balloon, and it will fly around.* Bottom: *Lift, thrust, weight, and drag are the forces that affect a plane's ability to fly and to land. To land, the engines must slow down so that the plane can slow down to reduce thrust and lift.*

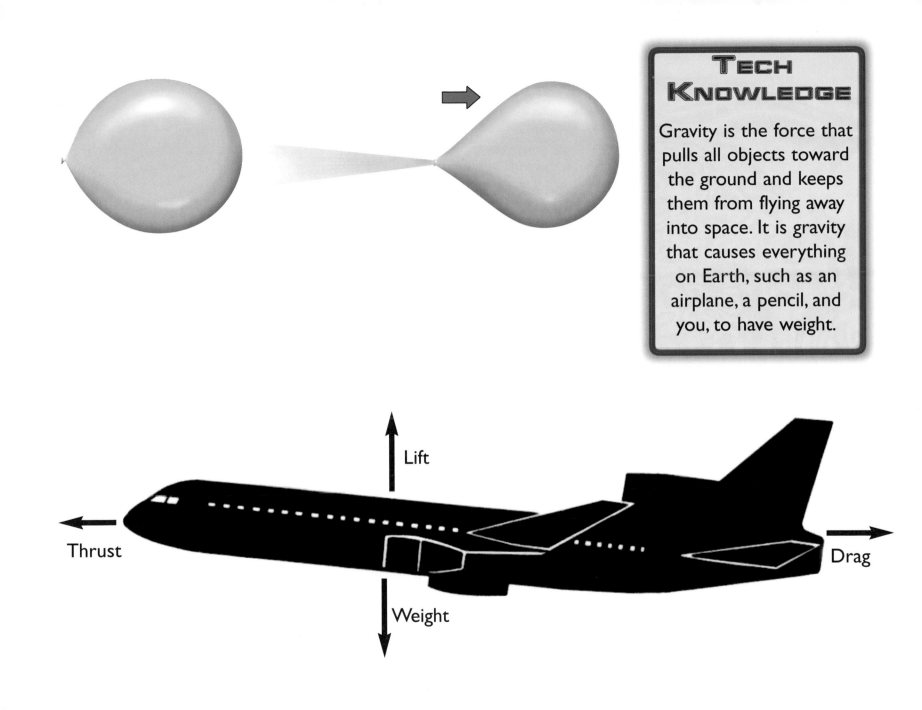

Lift

Thrust

Drag

Weight

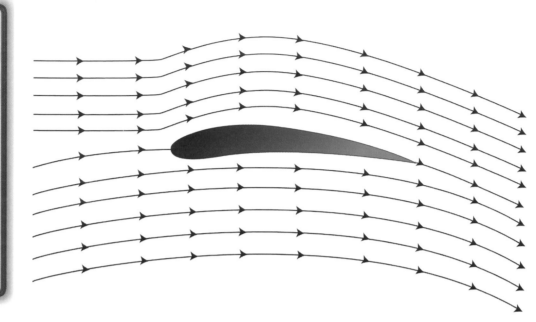

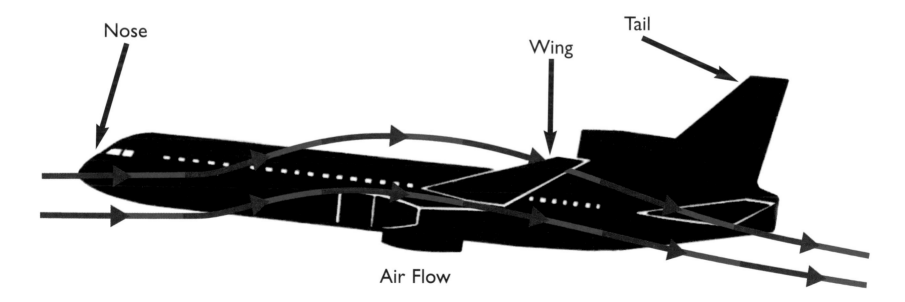

Nose

Wing

Tail

Air Flow

Wings

Airplanes need wings to fly. A plane's wings do not need to move up and down to create lift. They have a special shape that makes lift possible. The wings are **tilted** so that air hits the bottom of the wings and is forced downward, causing the plane to move in the opposite direction. As the wing forces air down, the plane responds by going up. The effect that air causes as it flows around the wing also helps to create lift for the plane. The top of a wing is curved. As air streams over the wing, it "sticks" to its top surface. The wing's curved shape causes air to flow downward off the back end of the wing. The air rushing downward off the back of the wing creates lift. This effect, called the **Coanda effect**, provides extra lift for the plane.

Top: *The upper surfaces of a plane's wings have a curved shape and the lower surfaces have a flatter shape to create lift. The curved top of a wing allows air to move faster and with less pressure over the top than over the flatter underside. The faster the plane flies, the more lift is created from the increased pressure pushing up underneath the wing.*
Bottom: *The wings redirect the air flow around a moving airplane.*

Flaps, Slats, Ailerons, and Rudders

Wings have movable parts that help them to do their job. Flaps are long, flat surfaces on the wings' rear edges. They can be raised or lowered to increase or reduce lift. Flaps and slats, the movable parts on the wings' front edges, can make wings larger by sliding out. This allows the wings to create more lift when the plane slows down. **Ailerons** are parts located on the wings' rear edges, near the tips. A pilot, the person who operates the plane from the **cockpit**, can raise or lower the ailerons by moving a control stick to the left or right. This makes the plane **roll** or spin. The tail wing has a rudder, a part that connects to the upright section of the tail wing. A pilot uses two pedals to move the rudder. To make the plane go to the right, the right pedal is pushed, and the rudder turns to the right. This causes the tail to move to the left, which makes the plane's nose move to the right.

Left: A Boeing 747's wing includes flaps, slats, and ailerons. Flaps change a plane's lift and drag. Slats change lift. Ailerons change the plane's roll from side to side. Right: To keep a plane steady in the air, a pilot uses the tail section, which includes a rudder.

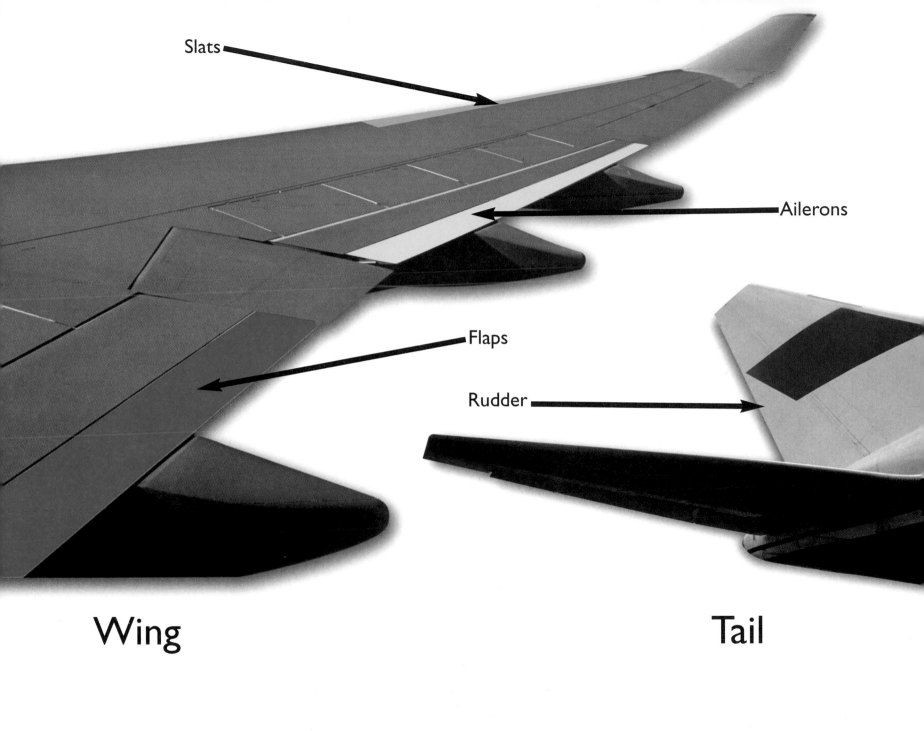

Slats

Ailerons

Flaps

Rudder

Wing

Tail

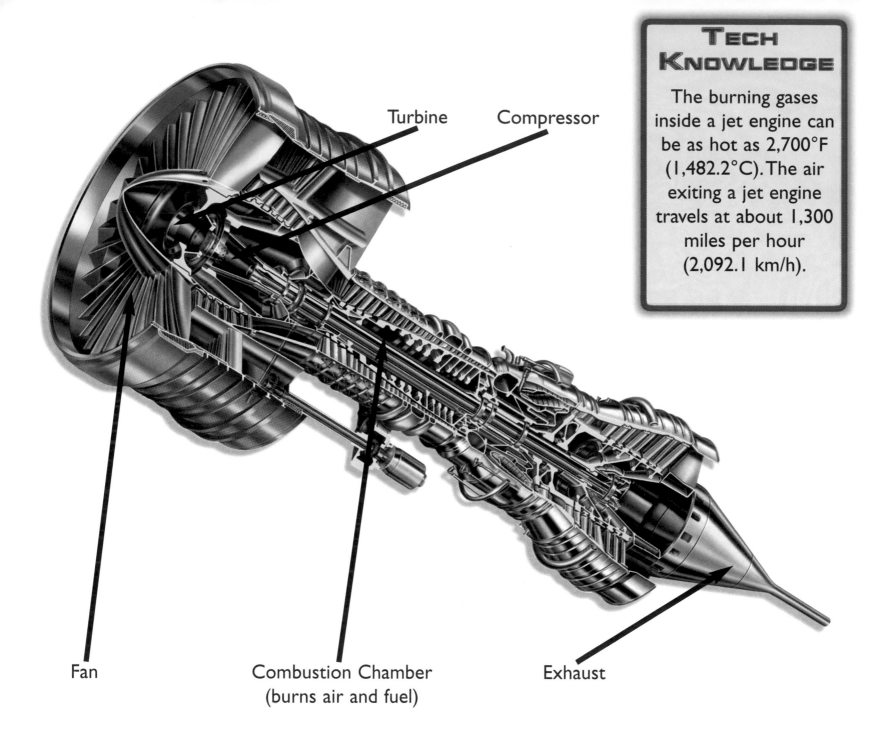

Turbine

Compressor

Fan

Combustion Chamber
(burns air and fuel)

Exhaust

Jet Engines

Have you ever filled a balloon with air and let it go? The air rushing out of the balloon causes the balloon to fly in the opposite direction. This is how jet engines work, too.

A jet engine is called a **turbine** engine, or turbojet. A fan pulls air into the front opening of the jet engine and splits it into two parts. Part of the air goes around the engine to the back, where it helps to move the jet forward. The rest of the air goes to the compressor, where it is compressed, or squeezed. Fuel, such as kerosene, is sprayed into the compressed air. The fuel and air mixture is set on fire with an electric spark, creating powerful, very hot gases. These gases spread out and blast from the back of the engine. This energy moves the plane forward. The energy also powers the turbine, which drives the compressor and the fan.

Large jets use turbofans. A turbofan is a turbojet engine with a large fan at the front to suck in more air, creating more thrust than a turbojet. Some of the air flows around the outside of the engine, which helps to make the engine quieter, and then flows out the back. The rest goes into the engine to create thrust, as in a turbojet.

The Concorde

The British-French Concorde, a special type of jet, has four turbojets. It is the fastest passenger jet plane in the world. It travels at 1,336 miles per hour (2,150.1 km/h). That is faster than the speed of sound, which is about 700 miles per hour (1,126.5 km/h). A jet that flies faster than the speed of sound is called a **supersonic** jet. The Concorde flies 11 miles (17.7 km) high, which is almost twice as high as other passenger jet planes. The Concorde's 17 fuel tanks hold a total of 31,569 gallons (119,501.7 l) of kerosene.

The Concorde is specially shaped to fly extra fast. It has a narrow body and flat, triangle-shaped wings called delta wings. Its nose is more pointed than that of a regular passenger jet. The nose can be lowered to help the pilot see during takeoffs and landings. These features reduce drag and increase lift.

Top: *Twenty Concordes have been built since 1969, but only 13 are in use today. A flight from London, England, to New York City on the Concorde takes only about 4 hours, which is about 3 hours less than flights on other passenger jets.* Bottom: *The Concorde has four turbojet engines. Fuel tanks are located in the wings and the tail.*

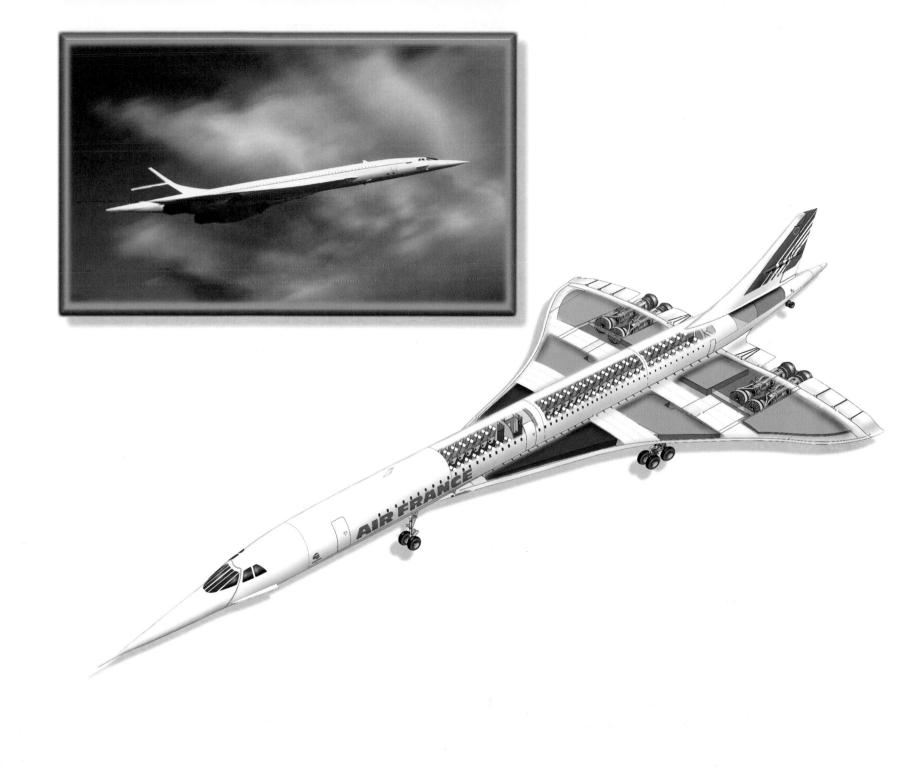

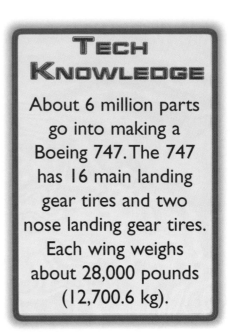

Big and Bigger

On May 2, 1952, a British company launched the first passenger jet, the De Havilland Comet. This airliner could seat 36 passengers. It was 94 feet (28.7 m) long, with a wingspan of 115 feet (35.1 m). The Comet cruised at a speed of 500 miles per hour (804.7 km/h).

Between 1953 and 1969, Great Britain, Russia, and the United States produced airliners as big as or bigger than the De Havilland Comet. On January 22, 1970, the United States introduced the Boeing 747 to the public. This jumbo jet was 232 feet (70.7 m) long and had a wingspan of 196 feet (59.7 m). With its tanks full and ready for takeoff, the 747 weighed about 710, 000 pounds (322,050.6 kg). The 747 had two floors and could carry up to 452 passengers!

Top: On July 27, 1949, the De Havilland Comet, the first passenger jet, made a test flight over England. The Comet is seen here flying nine days later. Bottom: A crew has to read about 75,000 drawings to put a Boeing 747 together. A 747's height from the ground to its tallest point is 63 ⅔ feet (19.4 m), equal to that of a six-story building.

Super Jumbo Jets

One airline company is trying to come up with new ways to make airplane travel more efficient. Airbus Industrie, a company formed by British, French, German, and Spanish airplane builders, is making jets even larger than the Boeing 747s. Called super jumbo jets, the Airbus A380s will be the largest passenger jets ever.

The Airbus A380 will come in several sizes. The largest jet, the A380-800F, will carry freight and will be 239½ feet (73 m) long. Its wingspan will be 261 feet (79.6 m). Each wing will have two turbofans. In one trip it can carry 150 tons (136.1 t) of freight, saving companies time and money. It will be able to fly 43,000 feet (13,106 m) high. The super jumbo jet will use less fuel and make less noise than do other jets. As a result, it will be less harmful to the **environment**.

Top: A possible cabin for the Airbus A380 includes a seat to let passengers stretch their legs. Bottom: The A380 passenger jet will have two levels to hold about 555 passengers. After testing in 2004, the A380 will be ready for passenger service in 2006 and will cruise at a speed of 630 mph (1,013.9 km/h).

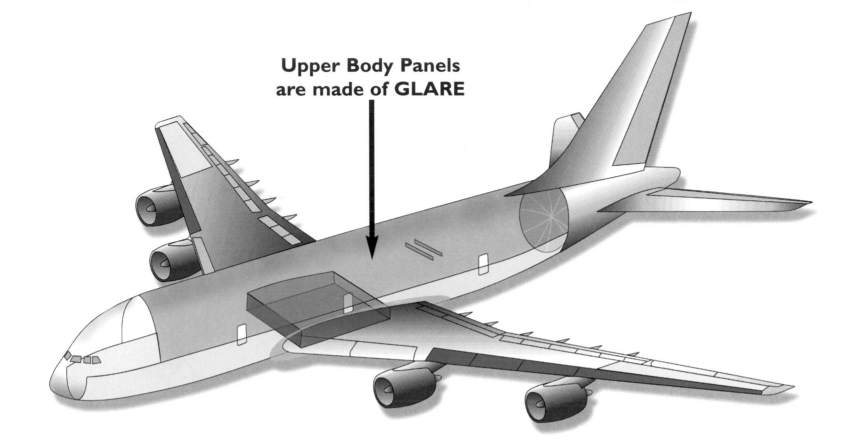

Upper Body Panels are made of GLARE

TIMELINE

Around 1686 Sir Isaac Newton presents his third law of motion.

December 17, 1903 The Wright brothers make the first successful airplane flight.

1930 Frank Whittle patents his jet engine.

1937 Hans von Ohain builds the first working jet engine.

August 27, 1939 Erich Warsitz makes the first jet-powered flight.

May 2, 1952 The De Havilland Comet, the first passenger jet, carries its first passengers.

March 2, 1969 The Concorde supersonic jet, built in 1967, makes its first test flight.

January 22, 1970 The Boeing 747 is introduced in the United States.

July 2001 Australia tests the first scramjet.

2004 Testing of Airbus A380 is to begin.

Let's Get High-Tech

Companies that make jets develop **materials** that are **high-tech** to make the jets more effective and affordable. Most airliners today are made from sheets of metal, each about ¹⁄₁₆ inch (1.6 mm) thick, called aluminum. However, the upper part of the outer shell of the Airbus A380 is made of GLARE. GLARE is a mixture that layers aluminum with glass fibers and glue. These thin sheets are bonded together, instead of being joined with metal bolts, to form a ¹⁄₁₆-inch-thick (1.6-mm-thick), stronger, sandwichlike sheet. Because GLARE is stronger, it is less likely to rust, will last longer, and is able to withstand higher temperatures. It is also lighter, because it uses less aluminum, does not use bolts, and has no seams. The GLARE sheets are welded, or joined together using heat, rather than bolted. The jet's engines will not have to work as hard as those on heavier airplanes.

Using GLARE on the upper part of the main body of the Airbus A380 makes the jet about 1,764 pounds (800.1 kg) lighter than using aluminum. Thanks to the use of such lightweight materials, the A380 burns less fuel and is quieter than other jet airplanes.

Jets of the Future

The Boeing Company is now working on a "flying wing." The Blended Wing Body, or BWB, looks like a single, triangle-shaped wing. This special shape will reduce drag and increase speed. The BWB will be 67 feet (20.4 m) wider than the Boeing 747. It will also be 71 feet (21.6 m) shorter than the 747. The flying wing will use less fuel than a jumbo jet does and will hold about 800 passengers.

A new jet engine called a scramjet might send passengers into outer space! A scramjet is a jet engine with no moving parts. Jet planes with scramjets will fly about 62 miles (99.8 km) high. They could travel from the East Coast of the United States to the West Coast in about 30 minutes! The BWB and the scramjet are only two of the ideas being studied by airplane companies. In the world of jets, the sky is *not* the limit!

Glossary

ailerons (AY-luh-ronz) Flaps on the rear edge of airplane wings used to steer a plane left and right.

Coanda effect (koh-on-DAH ih-FEKT) The action of a fluid sticking to a surface over which it flows. It is named for Henri Coanda, a Romanian inventor.

cockpit (KOK-pit) The space in an airplane where the people who fly it sit.

drag (DRAG) A force that goes against the motion of an object as the object tries to move through a gas or a liquid.

environment (en-VY-ern-ment) All the living things and conditions of a place.

high-tech (HY-tek) Highly advanced scientifically.

materials (muh-TEER-ee-ulz) What objects are made of.

patent (PA-tint) A document that stops people from copying an invention.

propellers (pruh-PEL-erz) Paddlelike parts on a vehicle that spin to move the vehicle forward.

roll (ROHL) The tilting motion of a plane when one wing rises or falls in relation to the other. Ailerons control roll.

supersonic (soo-per-SAH-nik) Moving faster than the speed of sound.

technology (tek-NAH-luh-jee) The way that a people do something using tools, and the tools that they use.

thrust (THRUST) The force that moves an object forward.

tilted (TILT-ed) Raised or tipped into in a sloped or angled position.

turbine (TER-byn) A motor in a jet engine powered by a mixture of compressed, or squeezed, air and jet fuel.

wingspan (WING-span) The distance from the tip of one wing to the tip of the other wing on an airplane.

Index

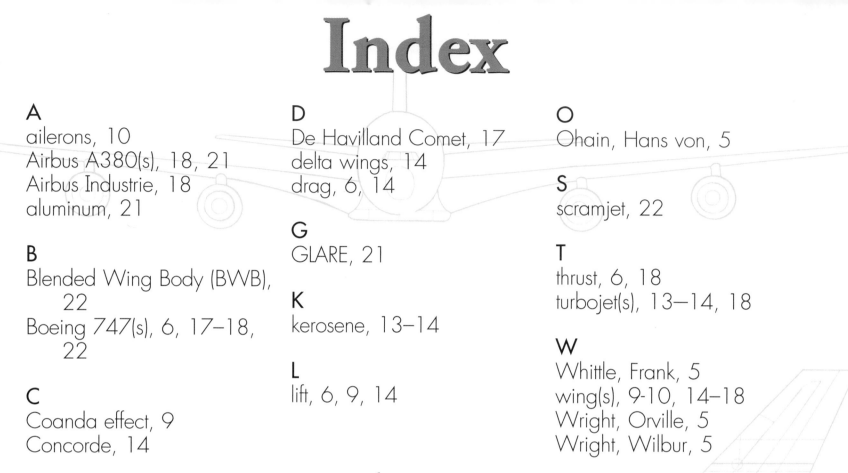

Web Sites

Due to the changing nature of Internet links, PowerKids Press has developed an online list of Web sites related to the subject of this book. This site is updated regularly.
Please use this link to access the list:
www.powerkidslinks.com/kgit/jets/